Hands and mouths and teeth and feet

MB MACAW BOOKS

www.macawbooks.com

Printed in India

One morning at school, Ginny saw her younger brother John fighting with another boy. She ran to them and shouted, 'Stop! Don't pinch and slap each other! That's not what your hands are for! Do you want to know what your hands are for?'

The children were curious. 'Then what are hands and feet for?' they asked. 'Well, hands are for snapping your fingers and clapping along to great songs! And most of all, hands are for clapping.' And so they all happily used their hands for clapping.

The next day, Ginny saw John and Lisa arguing with each other. 'Stop!' Ginny said to them, 'Don't shout and be rude to each other. That's not what your mouth is for!'

'Then what are mouths for?' asked John and Lisa. 'Well,' replied Ginny, 'Mouths are for saying good things. They are for smiling with. And most of all, mouths are for singing happy songs!' And so John, Lisa and Ginny sang some happy wonderful songs together.

'And do you know your arms are for?' Ginny asked John and Lisa. They shook their heads, puzzled. 'What are they for?' they replied.

'Well,' replied Ginny, 'Arms are for hugging!' She then stretched her arms, and pulled her friends into a big, warm hug!

A few hours later, Ginny saw Bobby biting poor John in anger. She ran to them and said, 'Stop! Don't bite each other! That's not what your teeth are for!' 'Then what are teeth for?' asked the boys.

'Well,' replied Ginny, 'Teeth are for chewing yummy food. They are for eating juicy apples and mangoes and grapes!' And saying so, Ginny and the boys bit into some delicious fruit.

A little while later, John kicked his foot against a rock. 'Ow!' he shouted, in pain. Ginny ran to him and said, 'Don't be careless! That's not what your feet are for!'

'Then what are feet for?' asked John. 'Feet are for running and hopping and skipping. Feet are for running races!' said Ginny. And thus, Ginny and her little brother raced to the playground.

Ginny and John soon reached the playground. All of their friends were there. The two held hands with their friends and sang, 'Ring-a-round a mulberry bush.'

Ginny was so very happy to be with her friends. 'This is the best way to use our hands, mouths, teeth and feet!' she said to them. What great fun they all had!

Then the children ran out into the streets, singing and dancing. 'I love to use my feet for dancing!' said John. 'I love to use my tongue for singing!' said Ginny.

'I love to use my ears to hear you sing!' said Josie.
'And I love our hands, and mouths and teeth and feet to have a fun time in the street!' said George.

At the end of the day, Ginny was very happy. 'How wonderful it is to use our hands, mouths, teeth and feet to make a happy day!' she said.

sharing is caring

One morning, Tessa was at the park. She wanted to sit down but all the benches were full. 'Come sit here! I'll share my seat with you!' said a nice girl. Tessa was so happy that she too decided to share her things with everyone.

At school, Tessa shared some sweets with her friend Tina.

'Oh, yum!' said Tina, 'I'll share my pen with you, if you like.'

And so Tessa now had an extra pen.

At the library, Tessa's friend Leslie asked, 'Will you please share a pen with me? Mine is out of ink.' Tessa replied, 'Of course, I will!' In return, the girl shared a toy hen with Tessa.

Later, Tessa met a little boy named Jonah. Jonah did not have any toys to play with. 'Don't worry, Jonah,' said Tessa, 'We can share this toy hen.' Jonah was so happy that he gave Tessa a large piece of cake.

When Tessa went to her friend Cindy's house, she took her the cake. 'Look what I got for us!' said Tessa. The two girls happily shared the delicious slice of cake.

'Tessa, I've got something to share with you too!' said Cindy. She brought out a large glass of chocolate shake. Then Tessa and Cindy quickly chugged it down together.

One day, it was snowing heavily. On the street, Tessa met a boy called Bobby. Bobby was shivering in the cold. 'Here, we can share my coat,' said Tessa. Bobby was so happy that he gave her his toy sailboat in return.

Afterwards, Tessa met a girl named Ginny. Ginny really wanted to visit the sea, and so Tessa shared her sailboat with Ginny. How happy Ginny was! 'Here, I will share my bicycle with you!' said Ginny.

The next morning, Tessa cycled to her cousin Joanie's house. Joanie did not have a bicycle of her own, and so Tessa said, 'I'll share Ginny's bicycle with you!' And so the girls took turns riding the bike through the neighbourhood.

In turn, Joanie shared her pet cat Fluffy with Tessa. Tessa loved to cuddle the cute cat. And what a great day Joanie and Tessa had, playing with their favourite cat in the world!

Tessa loved to share. And most of all, she loved to share her drinking mug with her best friend, Lily. The two girls always joked and giggled together over sharing chocolate milk.

Sometimes Lily did not have anything in return to share with Tessa. But Tessa did not like to share because she got many things from it. Sharing a hug with her best friend made her happiest of all.

Tessa's favourite part of sharing things was that it brought her closer to her friends. It also helped her share happy and enjoyable times with them.

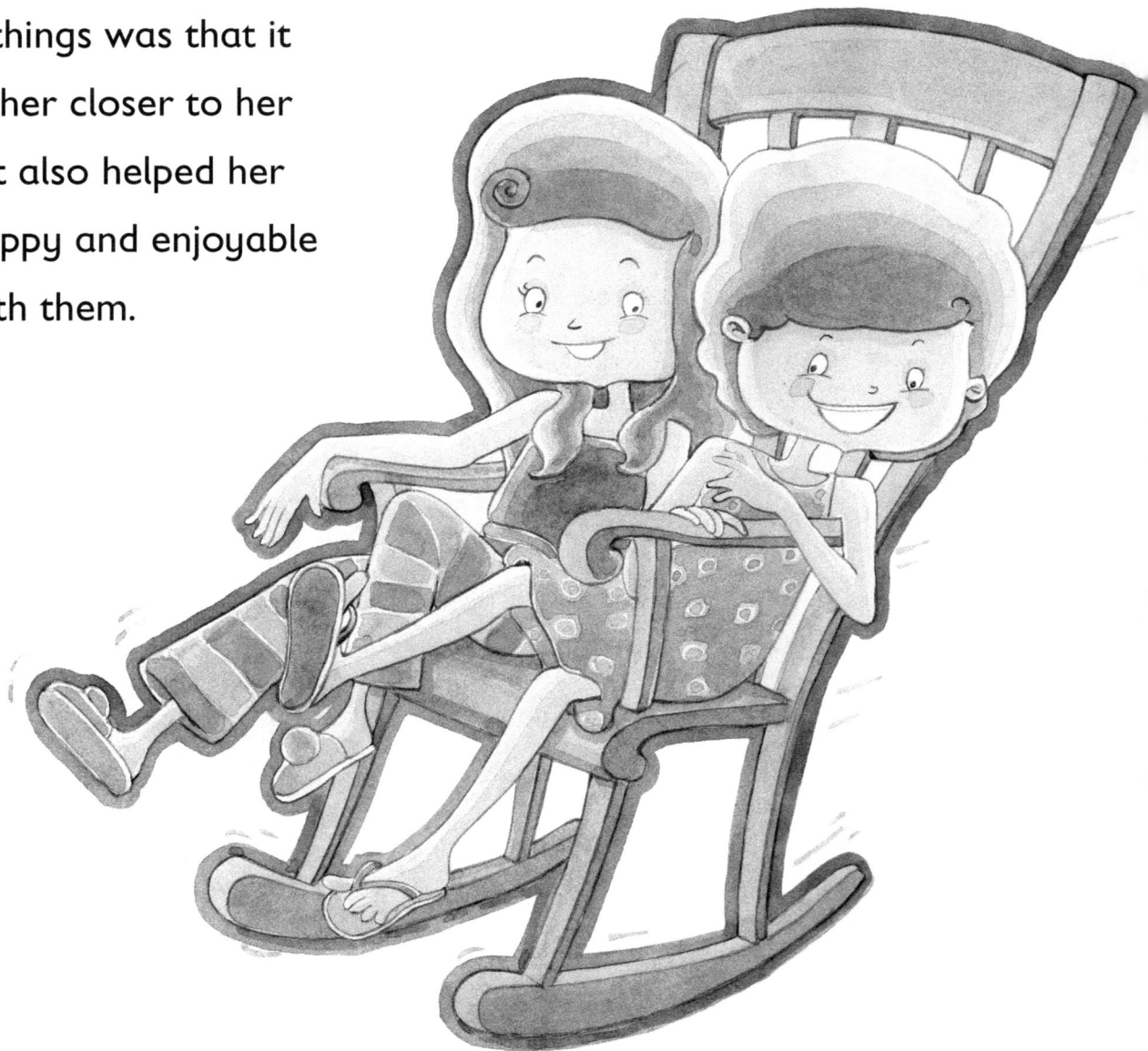

Tessa shared things with people because she cared about them. She was never selfish while sharing her things. t made her happy to see her friends happy.

At the end of the day, Tessa knew that as long as we all shared our things with each other, we would never fall short of anything.

www.ingramcontent.com/pod-product-compliance
Lightning Source LLC
LaVergne TN
LVHW082324080426
835508LV00042B/1532